Making the Team

A play by Meredith Costain

Illustrated by James Hart

Characters

(Chol could also read the sound effects.)

One winter morning before school

Ms Mackie: You children **do** love playing bat tennis. I've seen you play before school and after school.

Amira: And we play at lunchtime and recess.

Bree: Come on, everyone. Let's play!

Jake: I'm the best at bat tennis. I play to win! Watch this!

Jake serves the ball and Bree hits it back.

WHACK!

WHACK!

WHACK!

THUMP

Jake: Oh no!

Amira: Jake doesn't always win.

Bree: Especially when he hits the ball into the net.

Harry: Or out of the court.

Amira: Or misses it completely.

Jake: Oh well. You win some, you lose some.

The next morning before school

Harry: Hey, look! There's Ms Mackie.

Amira: Who's that boy with her?

Bree: I've never seen him before.

Jake: He must be a new student.

Harry: Maybe he's going to be in our class.

Bree: Great! I love making new friends!

Amira: I wonder what his name is?

Jake: Who cares? Come on, let's play.
It's nearly time for the bell to go.

Amira serves the ball.

WHACK!
WHACK!
WHACK!
WHACK!
THUMP!

Jake: Oh no! I missed again!

Ms Mackie and Chol come over.

Ms Mackie: Good morning, everyone!

Bree:
Amira: Good morning, Ms Mackie!

Harry: Hello, Ms Mackie!

Ms Mackie: I was speaking to you too, Jake.

Jake: Good morning, Ms Mackie.

Ms Mackie: Thank you, Jake. Now, I'd like you all to meet Chol. Today is Chol's first day at this school.

Harry: Hi, Chol! Good to meet you!

Bree:
Amira: Hi, Chol!

Chol: Hi.

Harry nudges Jake who is bouncing the ball.

Jake: What? Ohhh. Um, hi, Chol.

Chol: *(shyly)* Hi.

Ms Mackie: Chol is new to our school. Maybe you can show him how to play bat tennis.

Jake: Sorry, Ms Mackie. Only four people can play. And we already have four players.

Harry: It's okay. You can have my turn, Chol.

Chol: No, it's okay. I don't know how to play bat tennis.

Bree: I'll show you how to play. We can take turns. Bat tennis is fun. You'll really like it.

Chol: It looks like fun.

Ms Mackie: Thank you, Harry and Bree. That's very kind of you. I'll see you all in class.

Ms Mackie leaves.

Jake: We can't change players now. The scores are too close!

Bree: What's the matter, Jake? Are you scared we'll beat you?

Jake: Of course not!

Amira: Come on. Let Chol have a go.

Harry: Would you like to play, Chol?

Chol: No, thanks. I'll just watch for now.

Jake: See? He doesn't even want to play. Now let's finish our game before the bell goes.

WHACK!

THUMP!

Amira: Missed again, Jake?

Chol: I think the ball is supposed to go over the net, not into it.

Jake: Yes, I know.

Amira: We're winning now!

Jake: Just wait until recess! We'll beat you for sure.

In class

Ms Mackie: Good morning, everyone. We have a new student, Chol.

Chol: Hello. It's very nice to meet you all.

Ms Mackie: Tell us about yourself, Chol.

Chol: I'm from South Sudan. It's in north-eastern Africa. We lived in Juba, the capital city, but we've just moved here.

Amira:
Harry: Cool!

Ms Mackie: Now everyone, please help Chol to settle in.

Bree: Of course!

Amira: Any time!

Bree: You can sit with us, Chol.

Chol: Thanks, I would like that.

Ms Mackie: Harry, can you and Jake show Chol around the school at recess, please?

Harry: Of course, Ms Mackie.

Jake: But ...

Ms Mackie: Jake?

Jake: Yes, Ms Mackie.

Later, Jake is whispering to Harry.

Jake: It's not fair.

Harry: What's not fair?

Jake: Having to show Chol around at recess isn't fair.

Harry: Why not?

Jake: We have to finish our bat tennis game. If we don't, Bree and Amira will think they've won.

Harry: Does it matter?

Jake: Of course it matters! You want to win too, don't you?

Harry: Yes, but Ms Mackie said we should show Chol around.

Jake: Someone else can do it.

Harry: Like who?

Jake: Like Max and Ali. I'll ask them at recess.

Ms Mackie: Boys, get back to work.

It's recess at the bat tennis courts.

Jake: Where are Bree and Amira? I want to start the game!

Harry: Here they come now.

Jake: Bree and Amira, why are you so late? Recess is nearly over and we haven't started playing.

Amira: We were talking to Chol.

Bree: He's **really** upset.

Harry: Why?

Amira: He heard you asking Max and Ali to show him around the school.

Harry: Oh no!

Amira: You told Max and Ali you were too busy to show Chol around.

Jake: It's true! We have to finish our game.

Bree: It's only a game, Jake. We can play bat tennis any time.

Amira: Chol heard Max and Ali say they were also too busy to show him around.

Bree: Now he thinks no one likes him.

Amira: Or wants to be his friend.

Jake: Don't worry. We'll make it up to him in class. Won't we, Harry?

Harry: We can try. But I think we should start now.

Jake: Come on, Bree and Amira. Let's start playing. Where are your bats?

Bree: We didn't bring them.

Jake: Why not?

Amira: We don't want to play with mean people like you.

Harry puts down his bat.

Harry: I don't want to play either.

Jake: Hey! Wait! Come back! You can't all leave.

Harry: Why not?

Jake: You can't play a game with only one player!

Bree: Exactly.

Amira: You're so right.

Harry: Now you know how Chol feels.

Bree: Yeah. You're not being very welcoming, Jake.

Amira: See how it feels for a change.

Harry, Bree and Amira walk away.

WHACK!

THUMP!

Jake: NOOOOOOOOO!

Bree: (*pointing*) Hey, look! There's Chol!

Amira: Where?

Bree: He's over there, playing soccer.

They move closer to the game.

Chol: Grace, pass the ball.

Harry: Wow, look at those ball skills. He's really good!

Amira: He looks really happy!

Harry: I guess he found a team to play with after all. Let's go and join them!

Jake: (*running towards them*) Hey, wait for me! I'm coming too.